FOR PERSONAL USE

by Sunni Soper

Released May 2026

Printed in the United States of America
Cover Photo Michael Blue Smith
Edited By Jomar Valentin and Zach Howell
ISBN 978-1-7333152-2-7
Published by 310 Brown Street
www.310brownstreet.com

Sunni Soper

Sunni Soper

SUNNI'S HIERARCHY OF POETRY

LIGHT

WATER

FOOD

Sunni Soper

Poetry

Poetry is like church to me
I find God in these words and really
I don't know how anyone walks this earth without a little poetry

Haiku

Be careful what you
Say to yourself because you
Might be listening

Would you be friends with
Someone who speaks to you the
Way you speak to you?

Sunni Soper

LIGHT

Sixteenth Note

A sixteenth note behind my left ear
That ear may be deaf, but
My drummer is loud and clear
Rhythms quelling the silent screams from my upbringing
The ink bleeds into my ear canal whispering the secrets of ancestors
who roamed this backdrop long before it was blacktop

I watch blue birds painting with black berries on the whitewash of the
blackboard in my mind
The pictures they paint tell stories of different kinds
Stories of struggle and strife
Stories of love and life
Stories of husbands and wives
Stories of pain rife with teardrops of rain
Songs written from stains of strains in the vein of things that happen
everyday
Things that happen when I hold back what I want to say
When what I want to say manifests itself in myriad ways
Ways that hold my breath in
Like corset stays
Words tied tight in the crisscrosses of laces
Letters that never seem small enough to sneak through the eyelet
places

Music isn't restricted that way
The songs emitting from my marking speak
Whether spoken to or not
Painting pictures that make no sense, until they make sense
Speaking unfettered words left unspoken
Expressing feelings thought to be broken
Feelings full of hope
Fears
Opportunities up in smoke
Seized moments keeping my fire stoked
Burning through steel walls built around my heart
Steel walls that keep out the heal and hold in the hurt
Hurt that reminds me what it is to feel but
That hurt blocks my heal so

These walls must come down
Must
Come
Down
The beat of the music pounds the cold side of these walls with a rhythm that can't be turned away
Won't be ignored
Demanding a door to walk through
An opening to let oxygen in so my inferno can breathe
So these flames can seethe
Lick up the sides of my soul
Warm the spaces that have gotten cold
Remind me it's ok
Ok to live and dance to the beat
Leaked into my deafened ear canal by this permanent marking of ink
This magical sixteenth note

Sunni Soper

Fault

I'm loyal to a fault
If you didn't already know that
Then
You probably haven't reached the fault line
Where the tectonic plates of my soul and mind meet
That's not always my fault

Sunni Soper

Breathe

I try to breathe
But deep breaths don't come so easy when
My heart is stifled
Unrequited
Uninspired and...
Quiet.
I've never really felt anything like it
This feeling I can't quite verbalize
Even in peaceful moments that stabilize
I look into my own eyes
See the person in there
The one with so much to share, but
No one to share it with so
With pen and paper
I give birth to words that if not recorded
Turn to vapor
I step to the mic and lay myself bare
At the feet of anyone who may happen to care
I unzip my skin and
Pour myself naked

Sunni Soper

Skipping

Sometimes I skip verbs
Then
I
Don't
Know
What
I'm
Doing
Profound when
I skip nouns
Then
I
Don't
Know
Who
I
Am
I skip adjectives
Then
I
Don't
Know
How
To
Describe

this

Sunni Soper

Silence

The denseness of silence so tangible it caresses my senses with its appendages reaching through fog leaving me senseless
Awakening my defenses, condemning my offenses as it lingers and dances on un-mended fences surrounding depleted expanses of dirt roads driven in trances
Souls in transit, shedding the darkness
Searching for those with their likeness, alliance
Sharing a kindness that can only spread lightness
The denseness of tangible silence lets growth occur, unbiased
Learning new ways to do things, science
Standing tall against wrongs, defiance

Sunni Soper

Blindfolded

I put on my blindfold and went for a drive
Down the road and through the trees
I never felt more alive
Felt the wind in my hair and the vibrations from my radio
Seemed the lyrics were telling me just which way to go

Up this hill and around that turn
Suddenly a dip, I bottomed out, but there's still far too much to learn
I slowed down in that dip just long enough to feel the earth spin on its axis
Just long enough to hear the waves of the lake complete with ducks

The dips aren't always about scars from cuts
Sometimes you have to go low to truly get in touch
I've been down, and down this road before
This time, I'm definitely taking a detour

Not sure where I'm headed
But the car is filled with unleaded
I'm saving the leaded for my paper
Documenting words straight from my maker

My thoughts race at 170 miles a minute
A car honks
I must have drifted in my sea of contemplation
While going for a drive with my blindfold on

I hear the people searching
I feel traffic lurching

Start. Stop.

Start. Stop.

And with every start and stop
I start to wonder how many drivers feel their lives are a flop
I want to offer my blindfold, but I'm not done with my drive

I want to offer my vibrations, but I'm just not done with Isaac Hayes Live
At the end of each song I'm applauded for my Jedi driving skills
Applauding the fact that I've driven this far, blindfolded, with zero kills
Not even a one car accident, all due to my strength and will
Laser beam focus of all six senses directly on the wheel
The point is I SEE, I just don't need my eyes to do it

My thoughts race at 1700 miles a minute
Then a car honks
There I go drifting in my sea of contemplation again
While going for a drive with my blindfold on

As we all know, along this drive, things fall apart
Bridges crumble and roads degrade
So I turned my car around, blindfold still in place
Heading back the way I came, part of me must be just a tad bit insane
But there is molten lava boiling under this surface
It's ready to ignite, but the kindling must be perfect
I can almost smell the smoke wafting from the fierce, frenetic friction of my thoughts rubbing together
Thick smoke from hungry fires
They consume the paper from the top as I write furiously, just trying to keep up

All the while

My thoughts race at 17000 miles a minute
Auto pilot on, a car honks
I guess I drifted in my sea of contemplation
While going for a drive, down this road called life, with my blindfold on

Sunni Soper

Shattering Prisms

Barefoot stutter steps crossing hot coal bridges over deep schisms
Divides caused by choices in living
Traversable only via third degree burns and callouses
Hardening of the soul's feet
Equipment for this journey
Built-in shoes you can't forget
Scars that harden and protect
Trapping all the experience
Ability to reflect
Just barefoot stutter steps crossing hot coal bridges over deep schisms

Stutter steps of shuddering breaths gasped into frozen chest cavities delivering oxygen like provisions
Nourishment needed to carry out visions
Breaths that can become actions or prisons
Oxygen that can fuel or deplete
A necessity to combat defeat
Without it, you can't compete
Don't absorb it, and you're never complete
No journey begins with the feet
The steps only come when gases and passions meet
Nothing but stutter steps, shuddering breaths gasped into frozen chest cavities delivering oxygen like provisions

Breathing imagination in stutter steps of shuddering breaths of shattering prisms
The stench of burnt reality lingers
Each sliver slicing mortality
Filling the cuts with bleeding light
Showing the path to the unknown
A door never shown
A key all her own
Found in her jacket pocket, next to the lyrics of her song
The unfinished one with the broken harmony
Syncopated cacophony
No fluidity
Only the stutter steps of shuddering breaths of shattering prisms

Sunni Soper

Door

Words written in the grain of the wood
That can only be read by the light shining through the cracks
I read the words
Their spirit vibrates my being
My third eye seeing
The beauty before my eyes and society's ugly lies
For example, the worth of beauty and size
I sit back and analyze, retracing my steps
Trying to find what led me here
Soul bare and alone
Out of my comfort zone
On my search, I found a tool
One that's familiar, yet still shiny
It opens the door from the hinges
And lets light into the dark recesses of my mind
Places I don't go for reasons I don't say
It's been such a long time....

Sunni Soper

WATER

Sunni Soper

Haiku

You wouldn't say I talk
Too much if you knew
How long my voice was lost

Ghosts of Domestic Abuse

It's been 19 years and I still hear his voice
He's dead and his touch still haunts me
It sounds like a 9mm shoved in my mouth
It feels like praying my teeth don't break like my spirit
It sounds like being punched in front of a police officer
Sometimes it makes no sound like that vision in blue smirking and looking the other way
It feels like maybe he thinks I deserve it...too
It sounds like not calling my friends like I should because I don't want to bother them
I always bothered him
It sounds like crying alone in the shower so I don't burden anyone
I was always a burden to him
Sometimes I smile really big or laugh really loud and it sounds like "you look ridiculous" or "you're too loud" it sounds like the knuckles of a backhand busting my lip open so the next time I smile too big, it hurts, and reminds me not to look ridiculous
It looks like a restraining order written with lemon juice and no one knows to hold it up to the light
It feels like I'll never atone for the sins he convinced me were mine
It feels like I'll always just be too much...something
It feels like giving myself away and hoping someone will keep me…safe
It sounds like keeping to myself so I don't accidentally hurt anyone else
It smells like fear of wanting
It smells like smoke from past hopes engulfed in flames of disappointment
It tastes like not being able to form the words to ask for help

Sometimes ghosts come out in the day time

Sunni Soper

~~Victim~~

I tied down the letters in my lexicon that spell ~~victim~~ and
Forced them at gunpoint to stretch into the spaces that force me to embrace that I am a survivor
Present and alive for
All the things that come to lifers
Like hopes and dreams
All these things to strive for
All these blessings in the shapes of beings I would die for
Walking with the knowledge that He will provide for
Survivors.
Lifers.

You're only as strong as your weakest thought

Sunni Soper

Kiss

{an ekphrastic piece commissioned by San Antonio Museum of Art based on the painting Kiss by Dana Frankfort. Painting can be seen here: http://danafrankfort.com/gallery/2017_KISS_48.html}

He kissed me
Passionate
Messy
Blinding
Forceful
He meant it
Dana Frankfort creates layers of paint by scraping and sanding
Leaving a distressed surface that bears its own history
His kiss scraped and sanded my layers of protection
Down to my distressed surface and he started writing my new story
A combination of matte and high gloss finishes create the landscape for changes to come
I was blinded to his true nature hidden under layers of varnish
He kissed me better
He kissed away my pain

Then he gave it back to me
He questioned me
He accused me
I told him he hurt my feelings
He told my feelings they were lies
He refused to kiss me
I edited myself just hoping for a kiss
No matter how much of myself I removed
I still wasn't worthy of his kiss
I was blind to the fact that I never would be
I was punished
I still don't know why
His reasons were whispers carried off by the wind
Unintelligible like tree limbs on a window in a storm
Scratched out graffiti
He tried to erase me
He sculpted and chiseled as if my landscape needed reshaping
As if my topography needed editing, too
It was passionate, blinding, messy, forceful

Chaotic
Physical
Violent
He meant it

He said he loved me
He said he wouldn't do it again
Then he took a baseball bat to my temple
He tried to destroy my artifacts
He tried to scratch out my existence
He wanted to kiss me goodbye
He did it again
Bruised and battered
Sealed with a kiss

Sunni Soper

I Wear My Feelings on the Outside (2015)

I wear my feelings on the outside
Yes, I'm a poet, but right now
I'm talking about psoriasis
I've had it since I was 12
It used to cover 75% of my body
The treatments are worse than the disease in the long run
Don't worry, it's hereditary
You can't get it from staring or
A lot more than 125 million people would have it
No need to recoil and pull your kids close when I pass or
Refuse to shake my hand or
Refuse to serve me in your restaurant or
Refuse to let me in your fitting room to try on your clothes or
Refuse to do my nails or my hair or
Put my change down on the counter so you don't have to touch me
It's hereditary
I've been single for a few years now
I'm not sure I know too many people that can go years without starting to wonder if something's wrong with them
Close friends tell me I'm intimidating, so
For a while I told myself that was it, but
A recent date reminded me there is indeed something wrong with me
Something I forgot to remember
I decided to try the online dating thing, hoping my apparently intimidating nature
Wouldn't come through so much and maybe I could actually get a date
I chatted with some guy for a few weeks
He kept it light and respectful
I agreed to meet for a drink
He offered me the "AWESOME opportunity" to head back to his house where the drinks are...cheaper
When I declined
He told me I should be happy a man like
Would allow a leper like me in his home
That I should have disclosed I was diseased on my profile
It felt like having the dust rubbed off my wings
I wonder if I'll ever fly again
Now...grown up me knows this is HIS flaw, but
12-year-old me just remembers

Being bullied and cast out by my peers until I finally had to change schools, junior year
Feelings just don't reason
My feelings are exposed
Broken
Hopeless
Burdensome
Alone
The forgotten island
It doesn't matter how smart your talking monkeys or
How deep and clear your hot springs or
How pristine your beaches or
How expansive your trees or
How well your birds sing if
No boats come to your island
I guess all my resources just aren't so appealing once people see my feelings
At least now I understand…again...
I wear my feelings on the outside
I look pretty great from far away but
Now I remember why people just wave when they pass my island
Thanks for the reminder
I almost thought, for a second, I was just intimidating

Sunni Soper

Haiku

I could play you the
Broken record, but even
I'm sick of this song

I Wear My Feelings on the Inside (2019)

I wear my feelings on the inside
Yes, I'm a poet, but right now I'm talking about psoriasis
Exacerbated by stress
An outward expression of sadness
The first time I wrote this poem, it was about a bad date
Now it's about the date my psoriasis moved inside
To my bones
30% of the 150 million people with psoriasis get psoriatic arthritis
Rheumatoid arthritis' aggressive younger sister
She is that shitty roommate who never had her half of the rent
Wears you clothes without asking and returns them stained with red wine
Drinks all the milk you bought LAST NIGHT for your cereal this morning
She ate the cereal, too
She has company every night
Never does her dishes or cleans up after herself or her company
Steals your heels and breaks them
Except…I can't evict her
She lives in my body and her hobby is making fire ant mounds in my bones
She trains these ants in full scale assaults on my joints, at random intervals with no warning
My rheumatologist calls these intervals "flare-ups"
Expensive pharmaceuticals with ridiculous side effects manage this roommate squatting in my building
My skin is perfect for the first time since I was 12, but
Now my feelings are tucked away on the inside
Another side effect
My rheumatologist tells me most people go from diagnosis to disabled in about five years
I'm three years in and all I can think is I really might die alone now because who wants to date someone with fire ants in her joints and unpredictable intervals pressing pause on life?

Haiku

Just a dreamer
Slowly being suffocated
By reality

Cocoon

I used to worry that when this cocoon was through with me
I'd still be a caterpillar
I started spinning myself in silk after a little too much rain and ate a lot of Oreos so
I used to worry I'd just be a fatter caterpillar, but
I lost my appetite a few months ago and
I've pretty much been wasting away since
Now I wonder if there will be enough of me to emerge at all
Will I even have the strength to break out of this encasement I've woven to protect my encampment?
What do cocoons use for wings anyway?
I'm afraid it will need my hair, but
My hair is falling out and if there isn't any material for wings,
How am I going to fly...because some days...I can't walk
He said, "psoriatic arthritis" and I thought "how bad could it be?"
I traded Oreos for prednisone and blood draws
That was October 2015
September 2016, I put handicap plates on my car, they call it permanent

I still have more good days than bad, more
Happy days than sad, but
I give myself a shot in my stomach every 12 days and take a pill every night just to live my life at a pain level 3
At best

My doctor talks to me about filing for disability
I hear his voice, but I can't believe he's talking to me
Medical bills piling up and I worked so hard to get debt free
Then I think about that cocoon
Caterpillars liquefy almost completely to become butterflies
What if the way I'm coming together leaves me drowning in my own transformation?
Unable to pull myself out of my situation because I'm riddled with

inflammation
Nauseated from the pain
Reaching for a cane...
I never understood how people maintaining with chronic illness
consider suicide to be free from the confines of their disease
These days?
I understand.
I get it
Now.

Haiku

I truly thought quicksand
Would be a bigger
Issue in life. It is.

Submersion

Functioning depression is like a rainstorm with the sun out
Like a smile with tears rolling down your cheeks
You wouldn't even know if water wasn't left behind
Depression
Like an expensive string of Christmas lights with one bulb out
The cheap strings all go dark when one quits
Low frequency
Low functioning
Functioning depressives save those dark times for home
For safe spaces where they can remove the mask
You will see a hole in the light
It will lead your way home

Home

Depression doesn't want you to find your way home
Doesn't want you to talk about it
Doesn't want you to find your safe space
Doesn't want to light the trails of your tears
Reflect in droplets from your sun showers
It wants to be secret
We don't write about secrets
We put the pen down
We put the mask on
We smile
We offer kindness and help
We light other people's paths to safe spaces
We work to create safe spaces
We make everyone else comfortable because depression is uncomfortable
Trauma is uncomfortable
We wait until we get home to break
To shatter

We pray no one comes by to see our mess
To see when we are less…
Functioning

We take off our masks
Hide under the covers
Lots of covers
Between body pillows
Lots of pillows
Submerse ourselves in streaming services
Avoiding our streaming consciousness

We hope no one calls to snap us out of our submersion
I hope you call to snap me out of my submersion
I can't call
I am submerged
I am trapped in quicksand
I don't want you to try to save me.
There is no safe place to pull me out from
I don't want you to end up trapped in here with me
I can't lift this darkness alone
I can't light your path to help me
I have created a space where I am trapped
Safely ensconced in this glass box forged from sands of sadness
Indifference
Alone

My alarm rings
I haven't slept yet
I press pause on my stream of consciousness
I get up
Put my mask on
Go to work
Smile like all of this is fine
As if all my bulbs work
Like there are no secrets
And I function
I have kids
I have a grandkids
Giving up is not an option

Sunni Soper

Haiku

You take my breath away
I trust you to give it back
You do. In waves.

Deserted Island

I wonder if you're the type to come to my island and cut down some of my trees
Build a shack to live in with me or will you use my trees to build a raft and float out to sea
Leaving my island deserted
Again
With a few less trees

Sunni Soper

Haiku

I keep hoping but
My account is overdrawn
Hope is expensive

Hope Limbo

I tend to write when I'm hopeful or hopeless
Lately, I've found myself in a state of suspension
Afraid to hope too much because one more disappointment might break my suspension and send me off this cliff-side highway I careen as I give as much of me as I can spare and still function
This is a game of limbo
Or a state of limbo
Or a broken play button, stuck repeating the same song
They say the more you give, the more you have
What happens if you give because you don't know how to have?
Won't acknowledge your desire to have?
Afraid to desire to have?
Afraid you don't deserve what you have?
Have only had your haves taken by what you thought was the personification of hope?

I try not to pick up a pen too much lately because my pen knows me better than I know myself
Some kinds of hope come in ink form and I'm afraid I won't know where to find a refill
What good is a pen with so much potential if it runs out of ink and possibilities?
What if you only get so much ink, but you waste it on hopes and dreams?
It could be gone in a blink and then, what is hope worth?
An empty pen?
A passing thought gone before you get to the paper?
Gone before you find a refill?
Gone with the idea that hope is ever replenishing?
Hope is one of the most expensive gifts you can give
I don't know what else to do with it, so I try to give it whenever, wherever I can
I give it away
I want it away from me

I'm afraid to give it to myself
I'm afraid it will multiply
I'm afraid of the weight that settles when it's misplaced

So, I'd rather give it to you; you look like you lift weights
Weights of other people's expectations
Weights of your own expectations
You look flexible
Like you can contort your way under a limbo stick
How low can you go?
Maybe I shouldn't have picked up my pen
I hope I can raise the bar one day and end this game of limbo

Sunni Soper

She's a Dreamer

I'm a dreamer
Under the spell of pixie dust made from the ashes of cremated hopes
Clouding my eyesight
Forming apparitions on my irises
I wonder if I'm on your mind
I hope I am
I won't ask because those ashes remind me hope could end up more fuel for the fire and I don't know if I can pull myself from another inferno
I love hard
Completely
Unwaveringly
All in
I don't know any other way

Despite the soot
I still have hope
I hope my family and friends succeed and realize their dreams
I hope they all find happiness and peace
I hope they are surrounded by love, generosity and sturdy support
Me?
I have all those things already
But to share them..
To be wanted
Cared for
Needed
That's my muse.

Sunni Soper

Inside These Walls

I decided long ago that
No one else was allowed inside my castle walls...
I looked around and there you were...
I found you
There
Burning
In the labyrinthine twists and turns of
My smoky halls with sage filled urns...
I never wanted to put your flames out
I just wanted to warm my hands by your fire
Use your light to write by...
You know what?
Never mind.
I want too much

You were already inside my walls
I never wanted to cage you
I just wanted to be the one to help you fly
Be there when you land
I thought....
You know what?
Never mind.
I think too much
I trust too much, but
Now?
Now I have to put you with everyone else
Outside these walls
Lock this door from the inside
I wish you had just said something or
Rather
I wish I had just listened to all the nothings you did say...but...
I don't hear so well...
Above everything else
I wish I had realized how badly I had mistaken even our friendship...
Our closeness...
You know what?
Never mind
I wish too much

My last thought before I drift off
My first when I wake...
You know what?
Never mind.
I dream too much.
I guess I was dreaming when
You came inside these walls and broke up all my furniture
I'm sick of replacing furniture from careless men
Coming through my castle like tornadoes of destruction

I don't know how to heat the gold to pour into the cracks of my broken bowls to make them whole again
Or
How to repair splintered wood that used to hold our weight when we got up to our shenanigans
Or
Shattered mirrors with remnants of pauses in time
Pauses that recorded our rhymes...
I cut my finger cleaning up the shards and
I feel like...
You know what?
Never mind
I feel too much
And now I'm in here
Feeling
Too
Much
Inside these cold, lead walls
Just me
Looking at all this broken furniture in
These cold, dead halls
I need to stay busy
This mess?
This mess, I need to sweep
This one...
Wow...
This one cut deep

How am I ever supposed to let anyone else in!?
Inside these walls
With these vast, empty halls

Sunni Soper

Halls with echoes and
Echoes and
Echoes
Of your voice and
And your choices and
Now I'm hearing voices
They're giving me choices and
I'm making one.

Message received.
I'm finally done.
Moat stocked.
Door locked.
Shades drawn.
Drawbridge removed.
No trespassing for you.
Page turned.
Book closed.
The end.

Gifts in the Attic

I have a box in my attic
I used to open it all the time
Take everything out, but now
Every time I open it
I take out less and less
So
Now it sits
Perfectly wrapped
It took months to get the wrapping paper just right
More months to get the bow just perfect
These contents I feel too much to touch again, if I want to stay content
That box I know I can't open because
I don't have months and more months to get that paper and bow just right...again
What's in there needs to be in there, wrapped tight
Some feelings just need to be gift wrapped and put in the attic to collect dust
Never forgotten, just not given as a present, or in the present, or given presence
A gift I hide from myself because it hurts too much to untie that perfect bow or rip that just right paper
Opportunities to gift missed
This box filled with feelings
Sealed with a kiss

Memory

"Hey Sunni, remember that one time in high school?"
"Remember that movie? That tv show?"
"Remember that book we read in junior high?"
"How can you not know that song!?"
"Wait, you don't...remember...me?"

No. A lot of the time no, I don't remember what I never meant to forget
I had a head injury in '99, lost my memory and just didn't get it all back
People always want to know what happened with a whispered "Oh! I'm sorry. Was it a car accident?"
I'm ashamed to admit that sometimes I say yes
It's easier
People understand car accidents
Everyone knows someone who has been in a car accident

No, it wasn't a car accident
It was an accident though
I accidentally put my trust in hands with gloves spiked with ice picks that left black holes in my galaxy
Sending me on quests for splinters of time I'm not even sure are missing from my carpenter's structure

I was left standing alone on a beach
Holding an hourglass with a hole in it
Searching for trails of grains of sand like bread crumbs
Picking them up individually
Rolling them between my fingers as if they contain the Braille version of my story
Dating and categorizing
Carefully placing them in my new hourglass so they don't sift through the melted version of themselves...again...
I think...

I don't really know if I lost it or just found it
I don't even know what I don't know
Even my present is a melted version of itself
I have to date and categorize like a time librarian so I know how long it's been or when something happened or when something's supposed

to happen
but
This is not a sad poem about traumatic brain injury
This is not suffering from retrograde amnesia, this is surviving with it
This is reading nonfiction to unfold the neural plasticity formed around my past
This is scouring YouTube for music with my secrets etched on my scarring in the rhythm, the lyrics
This is buying more books than I'll be able to read in a lifetime hoping maybe the ink will jump off the pages and spell out my past
This is exploring poetry and letting poetry explore me
This is creating new memories and dating and categorizing them just in case my new hourglass decides to get a hole in it too
Then I won't have so much work to do next time I find bread crumb trails of grains of sand on banks of lakes with ripples from other people's rocks

Please always ask me if I remember something. Because I just might.

Sunni Soper

Caricature

I feel like a caricature of a character in a play
Scripted in the things I say
Blocking markers all over the stage
Like someone else is pulling the strings
Like I don't really know what it all means
But it seems
That I follow my blocking and
Say all these things but

I don't know where they come from
All these big ideas
All these eloquently phrased words
Combined to make sentences
Maybe this is my sentence
In this life of dichotomies
Clear confusion
Misunderstood comprehension
Deep shallows
I'm just sitting here in these gallows
Performing sentences written by ethereal beings with
This is my sentence
All eyes seeing
Gathering all these seedling letters
Growing sky high plants of words
Plucked and served sentences
Word salad for dinner

I say my lines
Blocking perfect
A caricature of a character in a play
I mean every word
Even though the stars write it
They hand me my script I learn
I'm not really in control here
Poetry oils my jaw
Pulls my strings
Directs my steps
Shows me how I feel things
I'm not really in control here

Sunni Soper

FOOD

Sunni Soper

Orwellian Capers

Just copped this reading material
The clerk called it a newspaper
All I see is a 1984 remix
2025 with Orwellian capers
The rights for the people taper until
All we are left with is vapors

Politicians are paid movers and shakers
Simply actors for corporate takers
Snakes with shark eyes
Reflections of dollar signs
Funding constructs of nefarious design
Programming the populace to resign
Resign all fight
Resign all rights
Resign all the light
Living in the blight
The American Dream just out of sight
They say it's just over the horizon
If you slave at this 9-5, you'll find it
Pay your taxes
Be a good little citizen
Their children are the only ones collecting dividends

Pockets fat from their fiendish ways
Endless lines of lobbyists all too eager to pay
Just to swing the vote their way
Six corporations control the global message
Six
Corporations
Brainwashing
The only lesson
Six
Corporations
Which one does your senator work for?

Buy our product
Take this charge card
It's just a little interest

We own you now
You'll just
Work your whole life only to die owing someone money

Sunni Soper

Bring Back Our Pens Response

After Christopher Michael's #bringbackourpens:

Christopher, I have these pens
I didn't buy them or find them
I was given them, divinely
They even came with two refills so far but...
I'm scared.
People lose their pens all the time
By the thousands and
I guard them with my life but
As they grow and learn about struggle and strife
It's their very life I worry about
Their ink sustains me
I would be lost if I ever lost my pens

#bringbackourpens © 2015 Christopher Michael
Persona Non Grata: poems by Christopher Michael

Sunni Soper

Haiku

Privatized prison industry's
Black ink profit line
Black on Black crime

Prison Industrial Complex

The complexities of complex imaginings birthed by the holders of purse strings
Strings that turn into shackles holding human beings
Defunding education to funnel monies to more restrictive leanings
You see
An uneducated populace is easier to misguide and control guaranteeing
Plenty of bodies to fill cages with slots just wide enough for coins made of blood, sweat and tears to fall through
Beds just big enough to trap dreams
Sheets designed to lock hope in the seams
The breaking of morale with ill-fitting clothing and
Food that rarely passes for nourishing

Corporations only care about profits
Prisoners are nothing but products
The human commodities of modern-day slavery
Corporate barons advocating for three strike policies
Donating to campaigns of candidates with "tough on crime" philosophies
Concerned more with occupancy rates than rehabilitative states
Concerned more with bottom lines than the impact of hard time
Recidivism is in their best interest so
They start them off early, paying judges for juvenile sentences
Profit margin growth without relying on interest
An inflation of the degradation of the family unit in this nation
Leading to one-sided teachings and nurturing complications

The insatiable thirst of this beast
Isn't bothered by its ripple effects in the least
Single parent families working several jobs with no days off for weeks while
The profiteers enjoy a feast from
Cheap labor on the backs of the meek
Unlocking the bars and calling them free, but

Still watching their every move and charging them fees
Just waiting for one slip up so their body can be counted again with ease
Can't vote, get a job or even a lease
Leaving very few options to provide for life's needs
Watch your step, one wrong move and the coins that jingle from your feet
Will land in corporate pockets to feed this iron barred beast

Sunni Soper

Haiku

Standing by during
Atrocities will make us
The accomplices

Bystander Effect

Trigger warning

1964
Kitty Genovese
Stabbed on a NY street
She yelled for help
No one noticed
She was stalked
No police
Then stabbed again
In her own stairwell
No rescue
Just trying to make it home
38 witnesses
Deafening silence
No help

I think about her as I stalk sleep
The way we can "that's not MY business" all the way to murder
Accomplices
Implicated in the crime of "someone else will take care of that"
Complacent
Kitty bled out while no one took care of that
They barely looked out the window
Complicit
Almost an hour of attack
Not one call to police
Almost an hour
We lost Kitty Genovese
Her death birthed the term bystander effect
There's a reason young girls are taught to scream fire instead of help
How do they look themselves in the mirror

2011

Raymond Zack
Alameda, California
Full beach
Water too cold for swimmers that day
Raymond
Standing neck deep
More than an hour
Mother calls police
Raymond is attempting suicide by submersion
Police and fire arrive
Claim they are untrained for these opposite conditions
Stand by
No one enters the water
Stand by
More than an hour
Full beach
Fire, rescue, and police
Still no one enters the water
Stand by
Coast guard called
Stand by
Raymond
Slips below the water
Finally
A bystander stopped standing and swam
He stood there over an hour
Finally someone tried to help
But it was too late for Raymond
Hypothermia
How do they look themselves in the mirror?

2021
Woman on a Philadelphia train
Name redacted
Clothes ripped
No one spoke up
Raped
Not one word
Several witnesses
8 minutes

Sunni Soper

Unused phones in hands
Video surveillance could see they saw
Still, no one called
Their hearts know they did nothing
Employee finally sees something
Says something
Police were there in 3 minutes
That's 5 minutes ripped from her by bystanders
A lifetime of awareness that people will just stand by

These are just a few of the broken mirrors littering this landscape paved with lack of intention
Lack of action
Lack of impact
7 years bad luck to anyone with the nerve to be victim
In public
With witnesses

See something
Say something
Look in the mirror
Don't be a bystander
Be effective

Sunni Soper

Haiku

Flint's undocumented
Facing ICE made with leaded
Water. Heavy.

Tree of Life

I used to be surrounded by my kind
Nothing but green as far as my branches reach
Sometimes I wish they had cut me down when they uprooted everyone around me
Too strong
They said
I will look nice
They said

We've been here for thousands of years and all that remains is me
I'm a symbol of life
They said
My rings aren't forming in circles anymore
My leaves hear whispers on the breeze of this place
They call it Flint
My roots are covered in sores and shriveling into my trunk
Branches brittle
Brown leaves veined with lead
Soon I won't be able to hold this ground
This soil is rotting from the deeds of rotted souls

I hear cries of acorns
Their mighty oaks afraid to soak up water
Weighted down by leaded ICE
Told they don't belong here
Told their identification is not native
I wish I could tell them they deserve life
They look no different from the native bushes that adorn my base
I was home base
Safe
Sustaining

My photosynthesis memory holds codes of a time when we all belonged here

There was enough here
Soil was fertile here
Enough clean water
Fresh air
Unimpeded sunlight
Now I have been infiltrated by chemicals I am unable to convert

Chemicals that settle in this dirt
Caustic and toxic

I'm not the only one dying here
They didn't bother to test the water here
I wonder if this place will be mentioned in history books for my seedlings
Or if it will be lost in a forest of other cities using substandard testing for their drinking water
Checking for undocumented immigrants at water pick up stations
Charging for water unfit for any living thing
This is financial martial law printed on documents manufactured from trunks of my beheaded ancestors
I am the tree of life
I am planted in Flint, Michigan
And I am running out of life to spare

This was written in 2017. Flint, Michigan didn’t get clean water until February 2023

Sunni Soper

Ramp
{an ekphrastic piece commissioned by San Antonio Museum of Art based on Ramp Painting #1 by Marcelyn McNeil. This painting can be seen here: https://marcelynmcneil.com/2018}

Open letter to gessoed backgrounds:

When I first look at this
painting
I feel safe
Served
Guarded
Proletariat progeny protected by purple poise
A blockade from the blight of humanity
A shroud of royal grace
And then I remove my white privilege colored lenses
Like lasers removing cataracts the image is transformed

Marcelyn McNeil uses chance, gravity and viscosity of the paint to create this work
Centuries of chance meetings turning to brutality created blood thick enough, the viscosity has turned blue uniforms purple
The gravity of this suffocates spirits left in their wake
A list of names so devastatingly long
The hashtags fade into a sea of grey

Gessoed backgrounds with thinned paints create the faded edges of our whitewashed history
Leaving us only a faded representation of Black voices
Their voices barely breaking through the white noise gessoed on the background of this country's foundation

The name of this painting is Ramp Painting #1
The police force in the south was initially established to track down escaped enslaved
Soon after the enslaved were technically freed
But this ramped up to the Black Codes, then Jim Crow
Now into incarceration disparities
Reckless state sanctioned assassinations of American citizens by an over militarized, under trained few
Rooted in a lust for power

This may sound anti-police, but it's not.
It's anti-police brutality

Consider the way Marcelyn McNeil uses her spatial awareness
Then create spaces for black voices
Be aware
Listen
Be open
Do your own research
Learn
Confront your inherent bias
Challenge your cognitive dissonance
Know you are climbing a ramp
Know you will lose your footing
Know you have to keep going
The people you are fighting for may not always be nice to you
Know you have to keep going
If they have to be nice to you for you to fight for them
You aren't there for them in the first place

There is a grace to the way McNeil lets shapes and colors unfold
Allow yourself grace to unfold into your future shape
Know you will still have creases
Work to iron them

Celebrate culture
Culture is the earth's palette
See color
You cannot have art without every pigment's gradient fading into focus

McNeil's architectural studies are evidence of the importance of
structural integrity to art
Reinforce the structural integrity of the Black community
Support Black businesses

People I love are Black
People I haven't gotten to meet yet will be Black
I worry when they're home
I worry when they're not home
They are not safe
Help me make them safe

Sunni Soper

#BlackLivesMatter

Sunni Soper

LOVE

Sunni Soper

Haiku

I forgot to remember
What I never meant to forget.
Myself.

You

You
My pen loves to write you
The way words dance off your tongue
The waltz when you woo me
The close and slow when you console me
A little B-Boy when you talk about your passions and
A jitterbug when you celebrate
My pen moves to write you

You
The way you walk
Rhythmic and intentional
Fashion unconventional
Unique, but professional

You
Have a sparkle in your eye when you get a new idea
Tear up when you see pain and suffering
You see right through facades
Invading other people's boxes of secrets by accident with nothing but a glance
Deconstructing their delusions of grandeur with one constriction of your iris
My pen sees you

You
Are intelligent and empathetic
Quickly bored with pedestrian rhetoric
Hungry for knowledge with a
Thirst that can only be quenched by truth
My pen loves to drink you

You
Shine a little too bright

Burn a little too hot
Most people don't know if they can handle you or not

You
Walk in your truth anyway
Unapologetically
The only way you know how to be
The only view you can see
Above these clouds
Chasing your dreams with
Passion pulling you apart at the seams into
Pieces of you
Y
O
U
Walking this earth and reading these stars putting pieces together
Star maps and moonlit paths the inky guide you need

You...
I hated that all my pen could talk about was you
Until I realized
This was all from my pen's first-person point of view and
The you my pen meant wasn't you at all
It was me
My pen sees in the dark and
Sees my darkness and still
All my pen can do is shine a light on the masterpiece that is
Me
My pen loves to write you

You
Me
I was so busy worrying about you
I forgot about me and
My pen was reminding me the whole time
My pen loves to write you and
Reminded me I'm a you, too
My pen moves to write you
My pen sees me
In pieces of you

Sunni Soper

M
E
Pick up your pieces...

Sunni Soper

Haiku

Found you with broken
Wings; I mend them knowing you
Might just fly away

How

Open letter from a bomb shelter:

How to love someone who is afraid to let you:
You will want to scream, but there is no point
Fear can't hear you
Plus...he's skiddish...so...
Screaming probably isn't a good idea

You'll want to read this poem to him
You probably won't
You'll want to tell him you miss him
Every day
You won't
You don't want him to run

You'll watch his mouth
Your thoughts will run
You won't register the words coming out, but his voice
His voice will slow your pace to somewhere between midnight and breakfast

You'll notice the way he touches things
The way he touches you
The way he moves depending on his moods

You'll melt when he looks at you
You'll love how you feel when he's in the room
You'll forget other people are in the room
You'll find ways to make contact with him
You have limits to how long you can keep your hands off him

Your friends will wonder what they see
You'll forget your friends are there

You'll leave early
You know you can't hide how hard you want to hug his pain
You'll wish you could hug him safe
Show him you are a safe
You'll want to hand him the combination

The numerical iteration to your highest walls
Your password

You'll pass words, leaving them unsaid
You'll wish you had the courage to say them
But you're scared, too
You've been through silver-tongued devils who sold you dreams that ended when the alarm clock went off, but you hit snooze one too many times

He woke you up
Breathed life into you
You'll want to show him love shouldn't hurt
Show him love doesn't have to be so hard
Show him you're a disabled landmine
That love should be fresh air
Showers of kind words
Encouragement
Teamwork

You'll realize it doesn't matter
You'll remember it may always be like this
You'll remember he may never choose you
Sometimes you take what you can get and sometimes what you get is more than you can take because he doesn't want to be taken
He doesn't know how to be taken
You don't really want to take him
You want to watch him grow
Blossom

So you leave him there
Water him
Love him from afar
Nourish his soul
Help him feel whole

Sunni Soper

Show him his beauty
Help him chase his dreams
You'll wish you were enough to allay his fears
You'll wish he would make space for your roots

You'll remind yourself these wants and wishes are selfish
Love isn't selfish
So you show him

Love is wanting to see him win
Whether you get to go to the game or not

Haiku

Never be with someone
You'd give up everything for
If they'd let you

Dangerous

I said you were dangerous and
I feel I should explain this so
You don't misconstrue
My interpretation of you
I can taste the words in your veins enough to
Know they came
From the same strain of stardust that
Makes me forget I'm
Afraid to be hurt

You're dangerous
I haven't wanted in a long time and
I want to...
Write the way I want to feel about you
On the inches of your skin
Nobody sees but you and me
With henna
Not permanent, but
There long enough that
You'll be able to see my words in your veins, too
You won't be able to look at your skin without reading my feelings and
That's dangerous
Because
Then you would know my feelings and
You would know my feelings are closer to
Permanent than temporary and
Let's face it
Permanent is scary

You would know that
It really wouldn't take much for me to fall
I don't know if you'd catch me and...
Part of me doesn't care
Sometimes I think

Maybe the fall would be worth it and
What if you do...
Catch me

I knew I was in trouble when I enjoyed your pleasure more than mine
I hear your words and
Say wow just as many times as when
You read my lips

They say loose lips sink ships and
While writing this
I can feel my boat listing
I'm pretty good at swimming, but
What if I take on too much water or
Find myself overboard or
What if the waves are just too strong this time

Time
Your ability to manipulate time as
Moments pass before I realize
The crowd I'm in when
You catch me looking at you
I can't look away fast enough
Another game of seconds

You're dangerous because
I don't like to come second
I just want to win and
I want to let you all the way in with
Reckless abandon, but

I'm pretty shy and
A little damaged
All I can seem to do is sit here
Watch time pass
See if my vessel finds its port
Maybe your stardust will make me forget
I'm afraid to get hurt and maybe...just maybe...
You'll let me show you
Your ship would be safe in my harbor
Tell me, what are you afraid of?

Sunni Soper

Haiku

Kisses on your neck
Keep my lips busy
So my whispers don't drown you

Eye Contact

Eye contact
I can't hold it too long
You'll see the secrets written on my iris
Like hieroglyphics on ancient papyrus
Languages of those who sired us
Communications of those who inspire us
Documentations of those we admire

My iris
Holding the unsaid like walls of pyramids
When you try to decipher
When you delve into my secrets
The room disappears
Just a few words in and I have to look away
Secrets so deep I don't want you to hear them say
All the things I never say
All the things that stay
On the forefront of my mind
Things that sit there and taunt me until I find
A way to tuck them away
Long enough to keep them at bay

Long enough for you not to hear them speak when
Your eyes meet mine and my brain skips a beat when
My heart pounds and my knees get weak when
My vision tunnels
And my blood funnels
From my head to my feet
I forget what was said
As everything disappears
All the people
All my fears

I get warm as
My emotions swarm
This whirling feeling has become my norm
As I sit in this uniform that
Hides my true form
I want to look you in the eye
Nice and long
But then you'll see the chapter that resides there
Etched into my irises
The incomplete one written from the first-person point of view
Because I only get pieces of you

Maybe one day
I'll let you linger there long enough
To read the stories contained in my corneas
So you can see what I see
The whole story

Sunni Soper

Star Seeds

Sometimes I stand outside and
Read the words in the clouds
Words that translate to sounds
Hoping maybe then you'll hear me
Through these
Translations from star seeds
From black holes where stars bleed
Maybe you'll hear how Greys bleed green
Or how things aren't really things but
You'll have to be fluent to filter through these communications
Convoluted transmissions
From undetectable originations
Filtration

Secrets between the dehydration
Begging for a touch of condensation
Hydration for the isolation of misunderstood translations
Hidden between palpitations that
Keep time like a metronome
Like the steps to get home
Stairways crafted with stardust

Until a disruption
A solar flare eruption
Shifting the beat of the palpitations
Another star seed's location
New messages revealed that
Were meant to remain sealed but
Now the secrets don't need to be told the
Translations in the fold are already known by
The one with the other half of the seed sown

With no need for translation or filtration there's
Condensation.
Hydration.
Star seeds growing star trees bearing star fruit and
Leading us all back to star seeds

Sunni Soper

Calm and Free

Come be calm
Be free
Come be free with me
Let me free you
From the burdens that weight you
The doubts that gnaw you
The fears that pause you
The pain that changes you
Let me make that pain functional
Let me define unconditional
Show you I'm medicinal but
Not really the traditional kind
I'm more of a light from my mind
The light you can't hide
If you just answer the door, you'll find
The only part of me that's trapped
Is the part you keep buttoned in your pocket
Pretty little pictures trapped
In a pretty little locket
Button fastened tight
On your front breast pocket

Come be calm
Be free
Come be free with me
Let me free you
From my pretty little locket
That I keep buttoned in my front breast pocket
Pictures I pull out and take stock of
Just a lot of
Frozen moments I'm not a part of
I'm there for some but
Always on the outskirts
Always mixed in with a sea of shirts
Nondescript but present
In the shadows, ever hesitant
Unbuttoning my pocket
Taking out that pretty little locket
And gazing at still lifes I wish were family portraits

Come be calm
Be free
Come be free with me
Let me free you
There are so many valleys with
Big shade trees and
Hills to roll down then
Crawl back up on our hands and knees
Pausing to laugh while dodging bees
Laying on a blanket as you read to me in a cool fall breeze with
Every possible moment seized
I wish this thought of that moment in time could freeze
I could transport there, just you and me
Dodging bees
You reading to me
Calm and free

Come be calm
Be free
Come be free with me
Let me free you
From the shackles in your mind
The ones that always lie
Telling you it's impossible but
I subscribe to Audrey Hepburn's line
The word itself says I'm possible
Be possible
Do the undone
Make more still lifes I'm not a part of
Shine like you're too big for the frame
Win all the pieces of this game
Check mate
Win
Just win and
Come be free with me
Let me free you

Sunni Soper

Don’t Love Me

Don't love me for my eyes, love my eyes for they see right through you, right through to the light that beams in you.
Don't love me for my lips, love my lips for the words that flow to the palette like paint for portraits of the future.
Don't love me for my voice, love my voice for the texture that caresses your energy until it takes form.
Don't love me for my smile, love my smile because it's free.
Contagious.
Don't love me for my hips, love my hips for the two jewels they bestowed upon this earth to beautify and harmonize.
Don't love me for my feet, love my feet for they have the strength to keep walking no matter how steep the hill, it's still. Left. Right. Left.
Don't love me for my knees, love my knees for they can bend down to pick you up when you fall and bend down again in prayer, making your next landing a little softer.
Don't love me for my nature, love my nature for its nurture.
Don't love me for the cover of my book, love the cover of my book for making you take it off the shelf and read between the lines.
Don't love me for this poem, love this poem for touching our candles, wick to wick, igniting a fire no water can ever quench.

Moonlight

I apologize for my visceral reaction to your offering of satisfaction in our most recent interaction but

You caught me off guard

A naked moment that revealed how
Moonlight spills across my collarbone
Raindrops crawl up the back of my neck
Sunlight runs along the inside of my ankle
When you look at me

Sun rays make their way up my shin to the den of iniquity within my pulse and
I want to put my mouth on you, I mean...say "Hi"

Scratched up like yard sale vinyl
You melted me in your hands
Re-pressed me into new form
Filling my cracks with a new norm
Needle playing a set of new poems
You make my surface smooth
Realignment of my grooves

You take my breath away
I trust you to give it back
You do
In undulating waves

How your eyes crest over the rise of the hills and valleys of my horizon's sunsets
Like twilight lighting the way to my climax
How I have to close my eyes so I don't overload
Like this CPU can't hold another byte
How my heart beats like it wants to be free from this cage
Like at this stage, it would be less painful to explode

I still can't breathe when you're around me
Or
I don't want to

Breaths pass time and I just don't want this time to pass

Sunni Soper

You Smell Like

You smell like the color caterpillar
Earthy and honest
Adorning my senses with rebirth
Painting sunflowers on my being
Brushstrokes of sunlight and raindrops
Solar flares blinding
Deafening thunder
I can't see you
I can't hear you
But I can smell your cocoon
Caterpillar
One day you'll bloom
Flutter your wings
I'll be waiting
For kisses
From the flutter of your butterfly wings

You smell like the color gravy
Hearty and homemade
Feeding my senses with wholesome
Sticking to my ribs
Fueling my adventure
Steam rising
Pan boiling
You burn me
I can't touch you
I can't taste you
But I can smell your thickness
Gravy
One day you'll come off the stove
And feed me
My soul will be waiting
For nourishment
From your consistency

You smell like the color opportunity
Open and available
Hopeful new outlook
Transcribing my future with fountain pens

Indelible
Visualizing my abilities through camera lens
Still life
I can't reach you
I can't feel you
But I can smell the air from your open door
Opportunity
One day you'll come to me
My stagnancy will be waiting
For the breeze
From your opening

You smell like the color music
Moving and harmonious
Choreographing my steps
Time signature steady
Beats per minute driving
I can't see you on my watch
I can't find you on a map
But I can smell your rhythm
Music
I'll be waiting
For your melody
To direct me

You smell like the color Sunday
Restful and calm
Laughing and clean
A burning candle
A book on the couch
I can't light you
I can't read you
But I can smell your relaxation
Sunday
Weekly you come to me
I'll be waiting
Six days
For you to release me

Sunni Soper

A Book in the Record Store

I am just a book on the shelf
So many topics in which to delve
Until at least fifty-nine past twelve
I'll be going much later myself

Pull me off this bookcase and break my spine
Maybe pour a glass of wine
Let's have a little sit down and spend a little time
Satisfy your starvation with my food for the mind

Notice the illustrations of faces
Your finger following my words, keeping perfect pace
Fold the corners of my pages to keep your favorite places
Write your notes in my margin spaces

Lick your finger to turn my page
What you're reading here are words from my sage
There's nothing left but to engage
Jump in my story and let's rampage

We can travel to places unknown
All while you stay home
As the flowers on the countryside of your mind bloom and grow
And the horizon comes into view as the wind blows

Blowing the words around in your brain space
Weaving a web of intricate lace
Making you go right there, to that place
That place that shows your emotions on your face

I'll put you in a trance until the last page
As if under a spell, cast by a Mage
I will make you my slave
As I capture you for days
And show you all the ways
You can get lost in my word play

I have so much to say
All you have to do is stay

I am just a vinyl record, take me out of my sleeve
Drop your needle in my grooves so I can breathe
Read my liner notes so you can see my contents, who made me
The list is long, a lot of folks involved
Listen to my songs, hear how I've evolved

Stories of trials and stress
Tales of love and survival
Get up and dance to me
A spiritual revival

A groove that can't be denied
A trance inducing melody
Everything vibes together, harmoniously

Time signature perfectly on time
Every song you hear, uniquely mine
It's all by design
Groove after groove and
Play after play
Hear the words between the lines you need to hear me say

I have so much to say
All you have to do is stay

Sunni Soper

Love you 3000

Every superhero partnership needs a headquarters…
A Stark Industries to Shield them from the multiverse

We will need more than one iron suit
More than one Quinjet
More than one Incredible Hulk of machinery to save this world with the only thing that's ever really worked…Love

We all need to eat
I know you like chicken
Let me lemon Pepper your Potts
Feed you in the castle you build to Asgard us
Sharpen your Iron…Man
The revenge to your Ronin
The eye of your Hawk
The Laura to your Barton
The multi-faceted infinity stones of our hearts

Speaking of hearts - Tony Stark's heart was built to resist the convergence of shrapnel
My heart was built to shield you from the convergence of life's shrapnel
If Mr. Stark could build me a heart to resist the onslaught of shards from my shattered dreams
It might be enough to resist the fantasies that remind me to breathe

But…
How do I resist peace?
Home?
He who lights my fire?
I'm no Johnny Storm
How do I resist the one my spidey senses when I close my eyes?
How do I resist the first person I want to speak to in the morning?

The most effective pain reliever I've ever found?
I'm no Wolverine
How do I resist that which I don't want to resist?
Not even a little
Not even an Ant's length

Not even a Wasp's stinger

Role playing is fun
Pretending is fun
The hardest role I've ever played is pretending I don't need Tony Stark's heart to protect me from the peppering of shards from the bomb of realization I'm not the same for you

Love you 3000

Sunni Soper

EXERCISE

Sunni Soper

Haiku

Try to make your words
Sweet when they come out in case
You have to eat them

This Rain

This rain makes my brain wander through flames and I always wonder if it's the stains from the pain or if I'm just plain insane.
Disturbed by the mundane way people go about their day never stopping to play the music their hearts say that could light their way even in the thick of the fray.
It amazes me how people walk around with their mind frames in the same space all answering to the same name and reacting to the same things with the same disdain, but very few take action to change things, reveling in the status quo of the same old same.
Too afraid of being thought strange to name names and see the game change and rearrange the deranged and estranged that make up the mass of madness contained in the fast lane gifting free reign to brain drain.

Sunni Soper

This Wine

I hate when I have so much wine that lines come to mind about how my lines line up with your intertwined thoughts combined with my insanely sublime space and time exposing our same kinds of lives and designs and deep exploration of mines and swinging from vines in jungles with no signs and troubles that are benign.
I'm a fool to deny the feeling inside, but for you to deny and lie to your inner fire and stop the embers that smolder from igniting a fire that could burn down the divide between your space and mine, a join that could be simply divine and defy all parameters of time if there was no wall to undermine the possibility of such growth of immaculate finery. Whether we sit in a winery or an oil refinery, the impeccable timing we create is uncannily divine when we combine our designs to remind the stars of our compounded shine complete with the ebb and flow of nature's time....oh when I have so much wine.....

Sunni Soper

Tossing and Turning

I'm tossing and turning as the words on my mind toss and turn to
formulate rhymes all designed by the crazy lines I hear each day.
Too many people don't think and take the time to find respectable ways
to express what they say and their words come out sour like limes.
Use your words wisely for in time you'll find they affect every thought
in your mind's eye.
Even if you try to block them or leave them behind they end up in your
pocket and travel through space and time on a winding road that can be
divine if you don't have to rewind and apologize for the unkind.
Words we use define us every time we make contact and recite finite
statements of expression leaving crumbs revealing the paths we take.
Some words reveal the love we make.
Some, the love we forsake.
Of the negative, watch your intake.
It can lower your stock and dictate your fate.

Sunni Soper

Radiohead

Kinetic Kid A, living Life In A Glass House with a Cinnamon Girl, never throwing stones, for fear it will collapse like a House Of Cards.
A Jigsaw Falling Into Place, they are Fitter Happier and Optimistic with Fake Plastic Trees, Dollars & Cents and Permanent Daylight.
She is his Melatonin, he is her Morning Bell and Nobody Does It Better.
In front of a tank filled with Weird Fishes, she tells him she wants to Sail To The Moon, he says "There, There, Go To Sleep, Black Star" to which she replied, "you're All I Need" and gave him a Lotus Flower that will Bloom when they say "Morning Mr. Magpie."
No more Fog, no more being left High And Dry, no more Climbing The Walls, No Surprises, only Big Ideas and a good old fashioned Punchdrunk Lovesick Singalong.
Packt Like Sardines In A Crushd Tin Box, they drive in their Killer Cars with a Paranoid Android and no Airbag.
I Might Be Wrong, but I think they're trying to outrun the Karma Police and learn How To Disappear Completely.
They Lift their voices and sing the Pyramid Song with chants of True Love Waits and Thinking About You.
They sing The National Anthem, but change the words to reflect The Trickster, the Rhinestone Cowboy, The Tourist, The Chains, and The Thief.
He stops the car, turns to her and says, "Being a Subterranean Homesick Alien, I Will Stop Whispering and use My Iron Lung to Sing A Song For You because I am a Rabbit In Your Headlights and with Everything In Its Right Place, Wicked Child, I am so Lucky I found you."

Sidenote: A Reminder, Anyone Can Play Guitar Inside My Head, but I've Seen It All and Pop Is Dead….cue Exit Music.

58 Song Titles

Sunni Soper

Rakim

To The Listeners:
Stay A While, you're just Waiting For The End Of the World anyway
Let's Teach The Children about The 18thLetter, The R
The Mystery of My Melody
This Chinese Arithmetic that constructs Lyrics Of Fury and Beats For the Listeners
Just A Beat to Put Your Hands Together
In The Ghetto you Run For Cover
Most don't Know The Ledge when they Pass The Hand Grenade
Rest Assured, these Casualties Of War are always the Finest Ones
Results of The Punisher, Keep The Beat and Don't Sweat The Technique
As The Rhyme Goes On this Extended Beat
Follow The Leader, I Ain't No Joke, follow me
It's A Must you see How I Get Down
I Know You Got Soul to Move The Crowd
So Let The Rhythm Hit 'Em and get Paid In Full
What's Going on? What's On Your Mind?
I know It's Been A Long Time but
I'm just a Microphone Fiend on a Musical Massacre so
I'll Be There, Remember That.

42 Song Titles

Sunni Soper

Prince Album Titles

Dancing in the Purple Rain, I let my Dirty Mind wander and cause Controversy around the year 1999.
I've been Around The World In A Day, saw a Parade go under a Graffiti Bridge throwing around Diamonds And Pearls like Mardi Gras beads.
Chaos & Disorder gave my Emancipation The Beautiful Experience, a Gold Experience even.
The Crystal Ball showed me The Sign 'O' The Times, the Truth of The Rainbow Children of Planet Earth.
Come, Lovesexy, it's all For You and your Newpower Soul.

20 Album Titles

Sunni Soper

Prince Songs

Location: the dream factory - number 7 Paisley Park Place

Outside
The timid ones walk by her number on the stairs
She stands in the Purple Rain
The most beautiful girl in the world
The secret of old friends for sale close to her heart
Darling Nikki
Headed for the breakdown of a rock and roll love affair
I guess she's got a broken heart again
Looks like another lonely Christmas

Inside
A place where breakfast can wait and Mr. Goodnight comes in with five women when the lights go down
Controversy and dirty minds are automatic
The insatiable are willing and able to partyup
The New power generation does the batdance for 17 days or until they get off
Endorphinmachines on the euphoria highway
Hot things and sexy mother fuckers wrapped in pink cashmere drinking pink champagne,
the gold standard in the halls of desire

A couple on the dance floor repeat the same moves over and over again
Showing there is joy in repetition
Elephants, flowers, starfish, and coffee
Kiss the floor littered with a litany of discarded diamonds and pearls

I headed to my office in the back of this temple full of thieves
uptown by Alphabet Street in Erotic City
Dorothy Parker's ballad seeped under the door
She's always in my hair

Rubbing two nickels and a dime together
I study a picture of Christopher Tracy in a little red corvette
A parade of girls and boys follow him under graffiti bridge

How come you don't call me anymore

I remember when you were mine
Thought you'd be forever in my life
The question of you
In the blue light
Indigo nights
so extralovable you made my sun shine
I wanna be your lover
I wonder would you adore me if I was your girlfriend

I twisted my chair to a new position
Took a shot of Anna stesia for my midnight blues
I need another lover like I need a hole in my head
I turned on the computer, the screen is blue
I forgot the beautiful ones broke that too

My neon telephone rang
It was a conference call from Chelsea Rodgers, Melody Cool, Annie Christian, and my sister
They said, "we're going around the world in a day in raspberry berets to hear what it sounds like when doves cry"
I said "take me with you
I need to get away from this pop life
I'm starting to get delirious"

I headed out under the cherry moon to go strolling over mountains in 1999.
I learned you just go round and round when looking for dance, music, sex, and romance.

84 Song Titles
Purple Rain release: 1984

Sunni Soper

D'Angelo

It's Alright, Lady.
One Mo' Gin I was Cruisin' Left & Right and with a Jonz In My Bonz, I Found My Smile Again, Me And Those Dreamin' Eyes Of Mine, while having a whole Devil's Pie, topped with Brown Sugar and a side of Chicken Grease at a Spanish Joint in The Root that is Africa, Playa Playa.
That's when I Feel Like Makin' Love, Send It On down The Line.

17 Song Titles

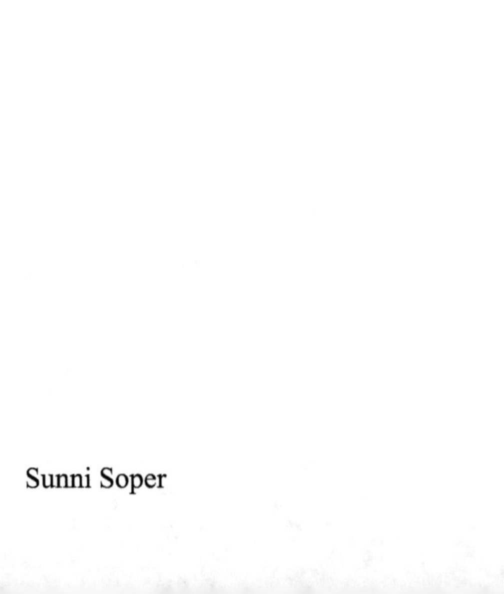

Sunni Soper

ENTERTAINMENT

Sunni Soper

The Unfinished Bookstore

I'm walking down the cobblestone street in an unfamiliar town looking for a decent cup of coffee. The buildings are a bit out of the ordinary, all seemingly based on various books. The mansion from The Great Gatsby, Wuthering Heights from, well, Wuthering Heights, a side-street that can be picked straight from West Side Story, and as I progress, there are many others that I can place from various novels, fairy tales, and stories.

Finally, I pass by a large building, it is unfinished, just a roof and walls with no paint, no finality whatsoever. This structure is literally just enough to be habitable with a small sign that looks to have been painted by a five-year-old that says "Coffe 5 cint..." I step into a tiny room and order my coffee, making a comment about the misspellings on the sign. The barista says "Yes, we know about that…it's unfinished."

Looking around at the unfinished tables and chairs, they appear as if Paul Bunyan himself cut the logs from behind the building and fashioned them together just enough to allow them to hold the weight of a person. I sit down at the nearest one, with my coffee, and start to sip as I begin to read the book that is already on the table.

Only a few words in, I look up from this tome to see a man come in, order a coffee and upon receipt, disappear behind a secret panel hidden by a bookcase. I rise from the table to pose a question to the barista. "What's behind that panel? Is there a fee to enter?" She answers, "There is no fee, only a desire to finish things." I told her how I love to see things finished and she hands me half a key and instructs me how to operate the lock to gain passage into the back room.
I enter this opening, thinking to myself "So, this is where the rest of the building is."

I look around the room lined with books, all with little pieces of paper sticking out of them. The floor is strewn with scraps of paper, pens, and paper clips. There are people all around the room, including the man who just entered, writing furiously, balling up papers and throwing them on the floor, only to write again. No one looks up as I enter, too engulfed in whatever they are doing.

I pull a book off the shelf and find a seat. Upon opening the book, I flip through to see that seventy-five percent of this book consists of empty pages. All of the little scraps paper clipped in the book contain suggestions for the writer. I think, "How odd, it's like a group editing process, except solitary."

I start to read, strangely finding that I have suggestions too. Compelled to share my ideas, I lean down and pick up an empty scrap, a pen, and a paper clip from the floor and start making notations of my own. By the end of this particular book, I have found that I thoroughly enjoy this editing, suggesting process, replace the book and take another. Taking, commenting, replacing, and taking another book goes on for several hours and a few cups of coffee from a cup that never seems to empty…I guess the coffee stays unfinished as well.

The next book I take resembles a biography of sorts. As I read on, I think, "How can one edit a biography?" A description catches my eye. It is a woman in an unfinished building, sitting on unfinished chairs, writing on unfinished tables, editing unfinished books, drinking an unfinished coffee. The description of this woman is uncomfortably familiar. The comments and suggestions are uncanny in their portrayal. Comments suggesting expansion regarding the scene in the coffee shop where this woman sits and reads a book that seems finished, but is in fact, nowhere near close. I continue to read, coming to the account of the woman's clothing, and realize the woman being described is ME!

I slam the book shut and race out of the coffee shop, the shadows are long now; I must have been there all day. This town has taken a spooky turn as dusk descends. I run with a frenetic pace, down the cobblestone street to the hotel I left that morning, storm up the stairs and into my room. Ensuring the door is closed and fastened tight behind me, I flop onto the bed. Staring at the ceiling fan, I wonder what kind of place this is and then drift off in a deep slumber.

I awaken back in my own bed, in my own house, with coffee that ends, and books that are completed. I reach in my pocket to find half a key, a paper clip, several scraps of paper, and a receipt I don't remember receiving for a five cent coffee

Sunni Soper

THANKS

Sunni Soper

Blessed

Blessed for the people
Blessed for the breath
Blessed for waking up
Blessed for the stress
Blessed for the sun, moon and stars
Blessed for the celestial rest
Blessed for the breeze that sets the leaves free
Blessed for the ability to hear the beat
Blessed to have ground under my feet
Blessed for curiosity and not mediocrity
Blessed for the sight to read
Blessed to have wants and needs
Blessed to appreciate the songs of the reeds
Blessed to smell the fragrance of the flowers
Blessed to recognize my internal powers
Just blessed

#MAKINGPOETSIMMORTAL

310 BROWN STREET .com

PUBLISHING

310brownstreet.com

@310brownstreet

www.ingramcontent.com/pod-product-compliance
Lightning Source LLC
LaVergne TN
LVHW010624100826
845148LV00014B/3105

* 9 7 8 1 7 3 3 3 1 5 2 2 7 *